TALKIN

CW00435344

Voices ɪɪᴏɪ...
the local
Liquorice Industry

Edited by
Sharron Cocker

University of Talk
Volume Two

Art Circus Education
1992

Published by Yorkshire Art Circus Education
School Lane, Glass Houghton,
Castleford, West Yorkshire, WF10 4QH

Printed by FM Repro Ltd. Repro House, 69 Lumb Lane, Roberttown,
Liversedge, West Yorkshire, WF15 7NB

Typesetting: Tony Lumb and Angela Wass at Art Circus Education

ISBN 0 947780 82 3

Editorial Team:

Ian Clayton	Tina Davis	Audrey Haggerty
John Hampson	Linda Malkin	Raymond Knowles
Beverly Lumb	Tony Lumb	Walter Marsh
Laurie Roberts	Elsie Sykes	Phil Paver
Reini Schuhle	Olive Fowler	Brian Lewis

Art Circus Education

Art Circus Education (ACE) is arts based practical training in an informal workplace atmosphere. It combines traditional skills like storytelling, writing and craft techniques with new technology and works towards an end prduct. This book is the result of this process. ACE is the education part of Yorkshire Art Circus, Registered Charity (No. 1007443). ACE is linked through its involvement with Yorkshire Art Circus to Wakefield MDC Economic Development.

Wakefield MDC (Economic Development Department)

The Economic Development Department is based at Cheapside, Wakefield, and has been responsible for the economic regeneration of the Metropolitan District.

CONTENTS

SUGAR

SPICE

... AND ALL THINGS NICE

We would like to thank the following people who have contributed to this book:

Sarah Backhouse	Alice Barker	Margaret Callon
Beryl Berry	Mary Betchetti	Gail Cocking
Margaret Carter	Betty Chambers	Wendy Day
Dean Charlton	Joan Davis	Nora Holdway
Grace Flynn	June Hilton	Brian Honeyman
Elsie Holt	Angie Hobson	Joan Lloyd
Judy Howson	Margaret Holt	Walter Marsh
Beryl Lumb	Jenny Idle	Christine Moorby
Ivy Millward	Linda Malkin	Neil Parkinson
Doreen Oaksey	Emily Money	Agnes Pocklington
Susan Parkinson	Ellen Parkinson	Andrea Richardson
Phyllis Ramsdale	Sandra Ramskill	Margaret Robinson
Amanda Rogers	Debbie Ruddock	Eleanor Ryan
Shirley Smales	Alison Stogden	Pam Stretton
Maureen Thorpe	Marion Tinsley	Tony Toole
Alice Vause	Ann Wakefield	Jean Wallace
Jack Walton	Pauline Wigglesworth	Hazel Wright

We would also like to thank Trebor Bassett Ltd of Pontefract for allowing students from Art Circus Education to tour their factory.

INTRODUCTION

A friend of mine mentioned the Art Circus to me. After an informal visit to the Glasshoughton building I decided to call again. I arrived the next Thursday morning to meet Ian Clayton and his group. They were discussing the launch of *PIT TALK*, a book they had previously written together.

I went along with them to the Disabled Miner's centre for the book launch. The members were friendly and enthusiastic about the work they were doing. I joined the group for the next project - *TALKING SPANISH*. Having three children, liquorice has been a common sight around my home, but I didn't realise the work that goes into making it. Working on the project meant visiting the factories. Once I visited Pontefract Museum to help in an interview being held there. Writing, cutting, editing and deciding how to put the marvellous stories in print, were all part of the interesting work the group did. People I know have said to me, "You seem so different these days, you've taken on a new lease of life."

Well it certainly keeps me busy. It helps to inspire amateur writers to open doors to the imagination and fires the spirit of those deadened by redundancy or years behind the kitchen sink. The Art Circus make a good pot of tea as well.

Sharron Cocker.

The roots of the Pontefract liquorice industry-Tom Glover

A PICK AND MIX OF LIQUORICE

In the licorice fields at Pontefract
My love and I did meet
And many a burdened licorice bush
Was blooming round our feet;
Red hair she had and golden skin,
Her sulky lips were shaped for sin,
Her sturdy legs were flannel-slack'd,
The strongest legs in Pontefract.

The Licorice Fields at Pontefract
Sir John Betjeman

The day they closed Bellamys down
tears and champagne flowed like the River Aire
Hazel Wright of Castleford

Why do people in this area of Yorkshire call
liquorice 'spanish'? The story goes that not
long after the defeat of the Spanish Armada, a
Pontefract schoolmaster was walking along a
beach on the East Coast. He picked up a
bundle of twigs washed up with the wreckage
from one of the Spanish galleons and thought
they might make good caning rods. Returning
to Pontefract he used these strange sticks to
mete out punishment on his pupils. In order to
stifle their cries the schoolboys started to bite
on broken ends of the sticks. The boys found
this plant to be sweet tasting, so that's why ...
And if you believe that ...

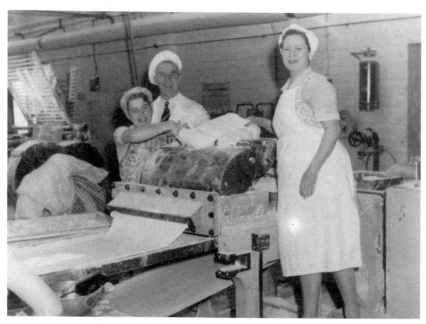

Feeding on the cream

SUGAR

It was all mother-daughter, mother-daughter

■ I was all set for going into the army after I left school until I got my feet under the table here. My mother got a phone call from Personnel. "I hear you've got a daughter leaving school, tell her to come and fill an application form in."
I was in the pea fields when my mother found me and told me to go down to the factory. When I got there they asked how many bags of peas I'd pulled. I said nine. Then they asked me when I wanted to start.
It was all mother-daughter, mother-daughter then; I suppose it still would be if there was enough work.

■ The most a woman could expect to be when I was there was a forewoman. All the spice factories in Pontefract were family firms so all the bosses were men. The sons followed the fathers and took over as directors. Some women didn't even have time to stop off and have their babies. They gave their lives to the firm but they never made it up to the management.

■ You know what they say about factory girls having a hard life, well, I loved it. There were seven of us girls around a table and we did have some laughs; chattered all day. Somebody would hiss, "Sshh, Mr Baxter's coming!" and we'd all go right quiet then crack out giggling soon as he'd gone. Friday night when we got us wages the whole gang of us would run up to Woolworths for silk stockings, sixpence a leg. Mam used to give me two shillings pocket money out of my wage; threepence went on spice, a shilling on stockings and ninepence for pictures. Saturday night we'd all go out with the lads to the Crescent or the Premier.
Alice, my big sister, worked at Wilkinson's, me and my twin used to help her out while we were still at school, selling Pontefract cakes in the park. It cost sixpence for one of them green tins. When I left school

9

Factory lasses

I started work at Featherstone's hat shop but that were only five shilling a week, not enough money for me. Our Alice said, "Come down to Wilkinson's. They might have you." I had to see Mr Harrison, the manager. Soon as he laid eyes on me he said, "Are you one of the twins? Haven't I seen you in the park?" They started me straightaway.

■ We had a boss at Dunhill's whose leg used to start shaking when he was riled. Everytime his leg went we knew what to expect. "Girls!" he'd shout, "Girls!" and his leg would be going like hell. We once sent some rubbish to Canada that had been swept into a box by mistake. You should have seen his leg that day.

■ I lacked confidence because I lived in Darrington. I didn't even go to the swimming baths, I just went to school. I'd have liked to have been a hairdresser, but I didn't have the courage. All my friends were getting jobs in the liquorice factories so I went to see Mr Archer. He said, "What do you want?"
I said "I want a job."
"Start Monday then!"
Just like that.

■ I had dreams. I wanted to be a nurse, I wanted to go in the army, I had brothers in there. I lacked confidence. My mother said, "No!", my father said, "Go!", and my brother said, "If you're a good girl when you go in, you'll be a bad one when you come out." I never went.

■ I wouldn't even dream about going anywhere else to work. Wilkinson's was the best factory you could imagine. It was hard work, I'll grant that, but we had some great laughs and there was a good social side. We even had our own works magazine. I once won third prize in a holiday photo competition held in it.

■ I used to decorate perfume bottles for Rockware, then I saw an advert in the job centre which said, 'Wanted; ladies with nimble fingers.' I've learn't since then; they don't just want nimble fingers.

11

■ We were never encouraged to do anything different. It was just, "Go out and get a job!" I always had a dream of being a nurse and felt that I should never have been in a factory - especially because I'd had TB when I was fifteen and spent months in a sanatorium at Knaresborough. My mother took me for a job interview at Robinson's and Wordsworth's, that was the Humber works. She said to the woman, "Can you give her a light job?" They put me on a little stool pairing liquorice bootlaces together. It's not the same as being a nurse though.

■ My big regret is that I never had either the confidence or the opportunity to do anything other than the liquorice works. There was nothing for us but factory work. Having said that, I never felt looked down on because everybody else was a factory worker.

■ I did retail training on the YTS scheme to work in shops. I put a form in for here and forgot about it. Then in June I came for an interview and I started in August in the mushroom department. I have done all my training now.

■ In 1949, when I turned seventeen, I left behind the low wages of the chemist shop where I worked to join my friends at Dunhill's. I was put onto packing, I loved every minute of that factory work. When I reached twenty-three, I couldn't see any future and I began to dream of joining the army. The lads would rib me about it. "Oh Eleanor, don't do that!" they'd say. But all my friends were married and I thought "I don't want this humdrum life anymore." So I joined. I met my husband while I was in the army. Later, in 1973, I needed a job again so I went back to what I was used to.

■ I didn't have a dream because I never had brains or opportunity. If you hadn't gone to grammar school you'd had it. There was nothing for us, only factory work. Everybody worked in factories. We went for the money. Children today have more opportunity.

It was like fairyland

■ One Saturday morning I went into work at Bellamy's. Disaster had struck in the night; a control lever had jammed and the sugar silo had overflowed. One of the lasses took me to the second floor to see the damage. It was like fairyland. Sugar had come out of the silo and had drifted everywhere making hills, mountains and valleys. It had even come down an iron staircase to the first floor. It looked just like a ski slope in Switzerland, with sugar mountains either side, or Iceland with Santa around the corner.

My supervisor gave Greta and me a shovel each and a pile of sacks. We were told to shovel as much as we could before our finishing time at twelve o'clock, and shovel we did, one shovelling, one holding the sack. At about ten thirty the production manager arrived. He was the second in command at our factory and had just been promoted from the Halifax factory. We were in awe of him as he was one of the big bosses. He had been phoned up about the leaking silo. He was moving house that day from Halifax to Castleford and must have been very busy. He took one look at me and Greta and the very large shovels we had and said, "You two hold the sacks."

He took the shovel and mucked in, shovelling like mad until nearly twelve, when he told us to get off home. He must have had loads of things to do what with moving and everything, but the way he mucked in he earned our respect that day, Greta's and mine. Oh, that all our bosses had been like him!

■ I remember Pizzey as a strong, stout, stern woman in horn-rimmed spectacles, wearing a blue overall and white apron. She was very active and seemed to spend all day walking round the factory making sure everything was running smoothly. Apart from one or two forewomen, she ran the place singlehanded. She had a powerful voice but we always knew that her bark was worse than her bite.

Pizzey would always greet new starters at the door and show them their jobs. My first job was pairing liquorice laces and sticking a label round them. I thought this was great.

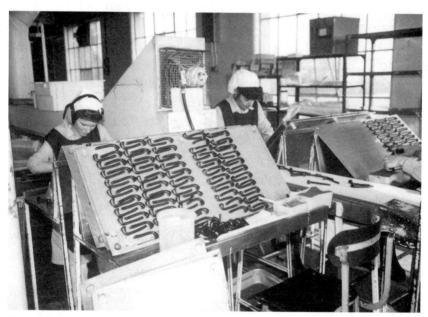

Pipe dreams

I remember one girl was dipping liquorice pipes into red sugar one at a time when Pizzey noticed her and said, "Nay lass, you'll have to be quicker than that, you want three in each hand."

The first day was quite an ordeal. The older girls would start asking questions like, "Are you courting?" If you answered no they would say, "Don't you bother with them?" If you said yes they would go on to, "Where does he live?", "How old is he?", "Where does he work?", "What's his name?" By the end of the day they would know everything about the relationship.

Pizzey encouraged some of us to learn making Pontefract cakes. "You'll have a trade; they'll always want Pontefract cakes" she'd say. Little did she know that they would eventually be made by machines and much quicker.

■ When I started at Bellamy's it was owned by Rowntree Mackintosh. We had an induction course in what to do and what not to do. We were given overalls and hats and taken down to the factory floor. I had never been in a factory before. After I left school I worked in a bank but then I got married and had three children in three years so we needed the money! There were about fifteen of us in the induction group and when we got onto the shop floor I was asked to wait at the bottom of the stairs, the others were taken into the new factory where the After Eights were made. Everything seemed bright and shiny there. I was very nervous when they came back for me and took me down a corridor, through a packing room, a cutting room and into the gum room. It was dim and starch just hung in the air. I thought I had been taken by a time warp to Dick's Days. They were doing jelly babies that day. I was shown what to do on each job around the machine. I was on weighing them when the redcap came up and said, "Do you want to go to the lav?"

I said "No, it's alright."

"Go on, go to the lav."

I again said it was alright; the truth was I didn't know where it was. She said ,"Do you smoke?"

I said ,"Yes." Then she insisted I went. Thank God someone showed me where to go.

I had never seen so many jelly babies in all my life. That night I woke up screaming, I had dreamt the jelly babies had sprouted legs and run me out of the factory.

We got mucky but we were all mates. The starch never bothered me, I suppose because as a kid I used to play at making mud pies. It could be uncomfortable though if a tray of starch went over you, it always managed to get inside your knickers. The new factory where I work now is more regimented, it isn't as easy going now. It was very easy going in Bellamy's but we always got our work done. I only meant to work there for six months, that's nearly sixteen years ago. If I'd committed murder I'd have been out now with good behaviour.

■ I transferred from Rowntrees' evening shift to Bellamy's afternoon shift. Eight or so of us sat in reception then one by one they all disappeared until I was left alone.

This little fella came for me and said, "Gail?"

"Yes," I said.

He then said, "You're with me, darling."

"God" I thought, "trust me!"

This little fella was Dave, who was well known for bottom pinching, I was later told. He took me down to the gum room where he was the supervisor. When I walked in I nearly ran because everyone was white from head to toe and the shift had only been working for fifteen minutes or so. Well, by the time he put me on a job I'd nearly worn me tights out as I couldn't stop shaking. By the end of the shift I was as white as everyone else, friends with them all and sure I would like it. It was a great two years in there. I was there until it closed down. Hard, mucky work but lots of fun.

■ I was bored stiff, wondering what I had got into. That changed when I was moved to the gum room. On the first day I saw thousands of jelly babies and nomps fall down this chute. I shouted to Red Hat Mary, "Mary, nomps are coming down!"

She ran over and said, "I know they are ,you silly bugger. They are going in the sander so you can feed on what you have taken off."

■ I started working at Wilkinson's in September 1963; I remember because Billy Fury and Joe Brown were all the rage. The first day they put me in the packing room standing at the top of a conveyor belt, putting tops on boxes. I looked at a box coming towards me and behind it was a phallic symbol made from a long piece of coconut rock and two small pieces. The long piece was in the middle. All eyes were on me to see what I would do. I laughed and picked it up, broke it up and shoved it in a box. My initiation test was over and the other girls quickly became my friends. As time went by and I got to work the machine I got my chance to do the same test on other people. I made one part-time worker blush when I sent a phallic symbol up the conveyor belt but she was alright, a nice woman. When I went to a function at the town hall and it turned out I had been working with the Lord Mayor's wife.

■ The first day I started at Bellamy's in 1955 it was awful, I hated it. I started at eight, went home for my dinner at twelve o'clock and cried all dinnertime. I went back at one o'clock till five and cried again. On Saturday morning my dad said, "Hazel, you haven't given it a chance." But it was the first job I'd had since leaving school and it was a different world. I told my dad that I'd go on Monday and if I still didn't like it I wouldn't go any more.

Monday came and what a difference; I got working with a grand set of lasses. We finished our work, swilled the floor, the machines were turned off and we could hear the wireless. It was all rock 'n' roll and we started bopping. I really enjoyed it and went home a different lass. I had some great times at Bellamy's. I must have, I'm still there 36 years on, and I've never had another job.

■ I hated working in the liquorice works, it was a swine of a place, every penny was earned in back breaking work. The forewomen were very clever and watched your every move. Tea breaks were only ten minutes long so if you were at the end of the tea queue in the canteen it was as well not to bother as the ten minutes would be up by the time you got served.

Working as a team

■ People worked in little teams when I first came here; there was pride then. You can take pride in a job when you work in little teams.

There used to be a big board up outside the factory gates and chalked on it in big letters was *"Hours arranged."* That meant women who had husbands on shift work at the pit could negotiate hours to suit them. A lot did the twilight shift - five o'clock till half past nine at night. What it really meant was that the women ended up with more work on top of all the housework because they still did all the snap packing and dinner making.

■ Eighteen months ago a new idea was thought up by the management of our new factory. On every line a team did the job, we weren't just workers but *a team*. Instead of a leading hand working alongside of us we were to have a team leader. The idea is that in every team, everyone plays a part. This is what was explained to us.

The team is made up of doers, the ones who really work and get the job done; the carers, the people in the team who care about the other members of the team; the thinkers, who can see better ways of doing things plus the team leader who pulls everyone together and gets the job done.

What a load of crap. In the old factory we didn't need new titles for workers, we all did our job. If anyone wasn't feeling well - their back was dicky, whatever - we helped out. If a job was finished quickly no-one sat back and said, "I've finished, sod you!", they helped get other people's work done. No-one finished until everyone finished.

■ There was one woman started who had been working in a shop but she left because she couldn't stand the women in the factory swearing.

■ First day I started I hated it because it was dirty. You got spanish all over you, if it wasn't spanish it was the grease they spread on the boards which went in and out of the hot ovens. I only stayed there for eighteen months.

My mother worked at the liquorice works, she was always the first there in the morning because she had a key to open up. As she opened the doors she would see rats running around the sugar bags that were stored there.

■ The first man on the job every morning was the man who fired the Lancashire boiler, stirring up the dying embers from the previous night's fire which had been banked up with no draw on. He had to clear out the clinker and soon had a good head of steam sufficient for the whole factory to function. Every department depended on two commodities, steam and hot water, so the boiler man had a very important job. As soon as he had steam up he would open the Ferrybridge Road doors for the seven thirty starters.

■ I came along to Wilkinson's round about the time of the 1926 strike and I eventually became the head pan man. People didn't like to work in the pan room, it was very noisy with all the pans going round all day. I had a cupboard with all my colourings in and I added them by using my eyes to know when the colour wasn't right. And I knew whether the mixture was ready or not, just by looking or touching. I didn't use a clock to gauge the boiling times, I knew when things were ready. If they weren't ready they'd have to wait. If the sweets were too sticky they wouldn't dry properly. It all comes with experience.

■ I worked at Wilkinson's packing when I was married, mornings half past seven while twelve. We worked on tables weighing sweets and packing them, you had to do so many dozen and the forewoman would come round to see how many you had done so there wasn't much time to talk. They certainly made you work at Wilkinson's.

■ I hadn't been at Bellamy's long when one day there wasn't much work in the gum room where I worked. So I was told to go to the spanish components department. Ecky thump, I thought, that sounds difficult.
   They showed me the room. I saw women sat at different tables; some were dipping pieces of spanish into a bowl then sticking it into stuff like hundreds and thousands. They were making 'pokers', others were separating thinner, long strands of spanish and tying them together, to

make laces.

They took me to a table where there were thousands of broad pieces of spanish in a tray. Close by was another tray of small round sweets with a clock face stamped on them, a bowl and a brush. I was shown how to brush the middle of a piece of spanish and stick the round sweet on. I was to do the watches.

I went a bit green at the thought of the glue I was using and asked another woman if it did your stomach any harm. "Nay lass," she said, "it's edible glue." Thank God for that, I thought.

After about an hour I was working like mad when a leading hand came up to me to take a look at how I was getting on. Suddenly she shouted, "What silly bugger has done this?"

"Done what?" I stammered.

"Well, stamped all these bloody watch faces with the wrong time, of course," she said. I felt myself go hot from my toes upwards. "They were on the table when I came," I said.

"The bloody lot will have to be scrapped, they can't go out with the wrong time stamped on em."

I felt all eyes on me and could have crawled under the table. Suddenly the leading hand slapped me on the back and started laughing and everyone joined in. "Sorry luv! I'm only having you on, we always take the mickey a bit with new ones."

There was a lot of laughter in Bellamy's, a lot of mickey taking but never in a cruel way. People liked to laugh with you, not at you.

When I first came here I worked part time in the cake room. I thought it was horrendous on the first day, I'd never worked anywhere as noisy. I'd been a wages clerk before I had my children.

I ate that many I made myself sick

■ You eat 'owt you can get your hands on when you first come to work in a sweet factory. My favourites at first were mushrooms and then sugar dummies. I once ate that many that I made myself sick and I had to go home. You don't bother with them after a bit though, it's like 'owt else you get used to it. Though just now and again when I go onto a job

21

Sisters in arms

I haven't been on for a bit and I'm handling sweets I haven't seen for a while I might bob one or two in my mouth.

■ There's not much pinching goes on these days. We might do the odd search now and again. In years gone by the lasses came up with all sorts to get stuff out. I knew one woman, I won't say her name, who tied that bootlace liquorice round her waist and took it out. She'd a figure twice as big going out through the gate as she had coming in. There was another lass who used to pinch sugar. She came from a right poor family and I caught her one day filling her bag up. When Mrs Hexby was here she used to have a little office and as the workers were going out she'd say, "Right, you, you and you," and they'd have to go into the office for searching. She'd have three or four in that little office every day.

■ A favourite way to pinch a few spice was to put them up your knicker leg till you got outside.

■ Edie Whitworth took over in the packing department after the war. She used to charge up and down a bit but she was always fair. She had some hassle from the boss though, he used to walk in and kick the dustbin over, looking for stolen sweets. Give her her due though, she would have a go at him, "What have you done that for, are you going to clean it up then?" she'd shout at him. She always stood her corner, did Edie.

■ I don't think the money at Haribo is right good for a man. It's okay if you are single but if you are married with kids it's not a lot. I think it must be okay for the women with husbands who are working. Generally in comparison to normal women's wages round here it's very good. Mind you I think we all work hard for it and we have to rely on bonuses and that to make it up.

■ Starting work at the liquorice works I got a wage of 19/6d a week at the age of fourteen and a half. It felt nice to have a wage packet which I gave to my mam. She then gave me 5/- back to keep for myself. I did a lot with 5/-, even saved a bit.

Wilkinson's factory seemed a massive place to me. With all the different departments it took quite a while to get used to where everything was. My first job was stripping sheets of sweets from boards ready to go to the cutting machines. Miriam was the forewoman. She seemed an old lady to me but I suppose she was only about 45 years old. She would often catch us behind the stacks having a good laugh. As a punishment she would make us strip the waste from the boards - an awful job. "I'll have you where I can see you," she would say.

I often watched Joan and Nellie making coconut rolls by hand and was so pleased when Miriam said I could have a slab to work on and practice making the coconut roll. I did very well and soon went on to piecework. I kept this job until I left.

■ One lady I know is 82 years old and she started work at Dunhill's in 1924. Her wage was 8/- a week. Later when it was 10/- they were offered another 2/- for working Saturday afternoons. She worked in the liquorice department near the stairs. When the entrance door to the factory opened and they smelled tobacco, they knew Mr Archer had arrived and they stopped talking or singing to avoid his wrath and sarcasm.

■ There were some days when I was terrified. You'd to do this, and do that, be quick about it; no dawdling. It was bad enough to start with and it got worse after. Mind you it was nearly as bad at home. I had to give my father my wage packet unopened and then he'd give me half a crown back, and he expected me to buy my own stockings out of that.

■ It was a very strict place to work. When you were working, you were working. When I left Dunhill's I set up as a vending machine filler-upper, putting cups and coffee in. I used to go to Dunhill's to fill their machine and I liked to stop and cal to the lasses. They weren't allowed to stop and talk so I'd be stalking mushrooms while I talked to them.

■ I worked in the spanish room at Macky's and I'll tell you this, you worked bloody hard. I never stood idle. I'd be washing walls or cleaning floors. And my mam had it worse. She was on piece-work and was only

24

satisfied when she'd made £2. She slowed down when she knew that she could bring £2 home.

Pontefract is similar to Turkey

■ People think liquorice occurs naturally round Pontefract but that's not right, it's actually a native of warmer countries like Turkey and Spain, countries where the soil is similar. Round here the root goes about three or four feet deep and then it pans out. It needs a good loam in the soil so I suppose Ponty has got a good loam. It takes some pulling up I can tell you. As kids we used to spend ages yarking it out.

■ I'm not sure if I'm right but I think I saw the last commercial crop of liquorice to be used in Pontefract factories being pulled up. I was on demob leave in 1946 and I walked down to Bubwith Farm on Knottingley Road, that's just on the low side of Water Lane. Mr Carter used to have a horse and cart and went round selling fruit and veg. I stood watching them digging and I had a talk with Mr Carter. I distinctly remember him saying "Well, that's it now, I'm packing in after this lot." By that time of course all the raw materials were coming from abroad.

■ Most of the liquorice that comes here now comes as extract from France. It's not long since it grew in Pontefract though. My husband's only 29 and he used to come here from Barnsley to get liquorice out of the fields. There was masses of it round here. Now the only bit that's left is round the flag pole on the lawn. I've seen people standing round it when they've been to visit.

■ I went to see a film show at Bassett's in Sheffield. They showed you Persia. In that country they don't dig the liquorice up like we do, they grab it out with mechanical grabbers tearing the plant from the root. In that way the root is left in and the plant strikes again.

■ The intake of raw materials came in steel barrels, seven to nine hundredweights each . When these arrived, despatch had to give a hand in the unloading. Come hail, rain or snow we were there. We used skids like they use for beer barrels to get them off the wagons. The full barrels were kept outside and in summer, when it was very warm, hessian sacking was put over them and kept constantly sprayed with water to keep them cool. Mr Marshall wasn't very pleased as the barrels looked unsightly and he made sure that the gardens and lawns were kept in immaculate condition. In the summer months, when trade was slack, we would be set on weeding the gardens.

■ I think Addingley's closed down in the 1920s and Dunhill's Tower factory in the late 1930s. The factories were used for stockpiling sugar during the war.

■ I left burling and mending in Pontefract, that was up Wordsworth Yard, where Brown's is now, to work at Hillaby's. You could just walk into a job then, not like now. Hillaby's was on Halfpenny Lane where Fells Carpets is. It was quite a small firm, with maybe about 200 people. I worked in the spanish room making those spanish wheels with sweets in the middle. There were about four or five of us on that job. We all knew one another because we had all been at school together so it was friendly. I didn't stop there long before I left to work at Ewbank's sweet factory which stood where Pontefract Hospital Day Surgical Unit is. Hillaby's got burned down later.

■ Ewbank's closed down in the 1970s. A lot of the lasses went to Dunhill's from Ewbank's. It was normal round here to work in the factories. You left school at fifteen and that's what you were expected to do, work in the local factory. The lads worked at the pit and lasses in the factory. It was the norm you could say.

■ A new factory was built adjoining Bellamy's, all new, shiny and stainless steel, not like our battered old machinery. After a while they gave us a cloakroom in the new part, but we had to walk through onto the shop floor, up the stairs and onto the corridor to get to it. We used to get covered in starch so we never wore good clothes to work in. The lasses that worked in the new factory didn't get mucky so they wore decent clothes.

The first day I used the new cloakroom I went up to the corridor and all the new factory lasses that were on the corridor suddenly flattened themselves against the walls. "What the hell are the silly buggers doing?" I thought. Then I looked down at myself and saw a blue overall with white starch all over it. They didn't want to get too close. I felt like a leper that day. After that I thought 'Sod it, they're only the same as me, a worker; the only difference is, we get mucky.'

■ Since Cadbury Schweppes took over we get called up to watch a lot of videos, safety videos and that. Some are to show you what Cadbury's are doing. They tell you that Trebor Basset is part of the sugar division of Cadbury Schweppes. They own Coca Cola as well. Mind everybody I know still calls it Wilkinson's.

■ When Rowntree Mac took over things changed but it took time. Bellamy's was a family firm; mothers, daughters and sisters all worked together there. When a girl came to learn the job from me I transferred all my knowledge to paper and when she took over the job, I went onto timekeeping.

Dunhill's girls

SPICE

I want 'em stood up like bodies

■ In the pan room you could hear the noise of the copper pans turning with sweets in them, and hear the people working as you passed through to go to the toilet but you couldn't see them for steam or sugar-dust. Everyone in there was covered in white powder. The floors were brick, hard and continually wet through. Everyone who worked there wore their oldest clothes for work as they were permeated with the smell of liquorice. People worked so hard there was no time for fun, it was a miserable existence. No-one looked happy so there are very few happy memories.

One young girl who worked in the cream room had three fingers chopped off in the cutter which cuts the allsorts into squares. She flung her arms around her workmate and said, "Oh, I daren't look!" She was then taken to hospital. It can put former workers off wanting to eat liquorice allsorts. Even though the smells were lovely, especially in the cream room, as the day wears on it can become nauseating. Some were even put off Pontefract cakes after seeing them being hand rolled prior to stamping.

One perk of the job was to be able to buy cheap allsorts once a fortnight, but not everybody bothered.

■ In the dinner hour I went to get a tray to stack the mints on. As I bent down to pick up the tray, one of the hooks on the mixer next to me caught hold of my sleeve. It picked me up and took me over the top of the machine. The pans were close together and I was jammed between the two. The machine, still turning, was cutting into my skin and pulling on my clothes. Luckily I was wearing rollers and the machine pulled them out instead of my hair.

I had been in the machine a few minutes, when Alice Palmer, at the end of the row, saw me. She shouted to Little Horace to switch the mixers off. He did and I fell to the floor, losing a lot of blood. I was rushed to hospital for an immediate blood transfusion. That saved my life. Everyone there was sent home due to shock. A week later I had to have my leg below the knee amputated. I remained in the hospital for three months and was unable to walk for twelve months. Another twelve months after that I went back to work in the packing department.

■ When we ran out of packing work, we would be sent to help in the mushroom department shoving stalks into the mushrooms. It was a job we all hated, we would push the stalks in any old how, but the foreman there would be hiding, watching us and would shout, "Stand 'em up bleeding straight! I want 'em stood up like bodies!"
Val would say, "Where the bloody hell is he shouting from?"

■ I had been working at Wilkinson's about three days in the cutting room, cutting the liquorice sandwiches into allsorts. I had been working for a while when suddenly a voice came booming over the tannoy, "Who's that girl working without an overall and hat?" I looked up to find everyone looking at me. I was so embarrassed,
I had to see the manager in his office and when I told him I'd only been there three days and hadn't been given a uniform, he apologised. I went home that dinner time and didn't go back until I got my uniform. I only worked there about six months and didn't really like it.

■ Mr Archer was the manager and word used to go around when he was coming. Everyone would scurry around and find something to do to look busy.

■ Once I remember, it would be after the war, when ex-soldiers were coming back, we were singing a Jessie Matthew's song and someone shouted, "Hey up! Archer's coming." This kid said, "We tell him what to do now not the other way round."

■ What a lot of changes! On Friday afternoons Bertie Bellamy would come down and get two girls to wash his car. You never get jobs in the factory like that now.

The tricks we used to get up to in the pan room! There were five bays and a male boss on each bay. We waited while they went to the loo then we sewed their coat cuffs and trouser bottoms together. What a laugh at home time when they tried to get dressed.

My boss lived next door and he used to come to work with his wife's woollen blankets, saying "We can't get the washing dry. Hang them up in the stoves," It was like a launderette. Our boss in the pan room had a stiff leg and, morning and night when he came to change his shoes, Annie Malcolm used to fasten his shoe for him. He bought her a present every year as he appreciated it. The day Bellamy's closed down the tears and champagne flowed like the River Aire.

■ Haribo is a German firm. I think two brothers started the firm in Bonn, one was a chemist. They have factories all over Europe now. The Godsons owned the factory when it was Dunhill's and they are directors with Haribo now. I think the name Haribo in some way comes from the name of the brothers who started the firm, and their home town; Henry Regal from Bonn.

Haribo have put money into the firm and expanded the building, so they must be one of the biggest employers in Pontefract now. The firm is interested in competing on the European market.

■ Haribo means efficiency. When a big German comes over everything is brushed and spotless. But I bet if I went to Germany and told them I worked at the English factory they wouldn't let me look round. ·

■ Before that it was all old machines where I worked, all old conkers. The floors were very slippy but they are all bricked and slicked now.

■ We had great fun in the pan room. Eight of us worked in a team. There was Jessie Brain and Renee Richardson, they're both dead now, bless 'em. We used to watch for each other coming and clock each other on. You might get the sack for doing that now at Haribo.

■ Many years ago I used to be a Pontefract cake stamper. They have a machine now to do what I did, I wonder how many it can make in an

31

Stamping

hour? I had to do twelve dozen trays an hour in my day. We had a supply of tins, as we called them - they were big trays really - and the first job was to grease the tins to stop the cakes sticking. I'd grab a lump of black paste and knead it and roll it until it was just right to be cut into little pieces, enough to make one cake. I'd put the blobs onto the tray, about 240 in each, as fast as I could. Then after a quick flattening with my hand, I'd pick up my stamper and I'd have a tray stamped in no time. Then I'd put the tray onto a drying table where it dried all night, and start again. By we were quick in them days!

The next day a stripper would scrape off the cakes with an aluminium scraper and pack them into boxes. The tins would then be washed ready to be filled up again.

■ At Haribo it's more or less all machines now. The machines do all the packing and it's not really hard to do the jobs, you just get tired from being there all day I suppose.

■ The stacks of trays in the gum room were about 6'6" tall. Many a top tray has been pulled over the person who has been taking it off to put in the machine, and left them with a pure white face through which only their eyes showed. When a tray got stuck in the machine, the supervisor had to climb about four feet off the ground, on top of the machine, take off a cover and, lying on the top of the machine, reach down and free the tray. One day the tray was stuck so deep that his head and shoulders disappeared into the machine. Then he had to wriggle even further in until only his legs were showing. He did look funny with his legs waving about, the rest of him inside the machine. Still it gave us a ten minute break.

■ I worked in the spanish room for twelve months before I left to have a baby. I was a conveyor belt worker and there were four machines in the room. There was a girl sitting behind the feeder machine cutting big lumps of raw liquorice and putting it into the feeder. She had to push it into the feeder really hard and your arm had to go into the machine. The machine was constantly twisting and you had to watch that you didn't get your arm twisted whilst the machine was working. If you worked on the feeder you got paid more because it was dangerous.

As the raw liquorice was pressed through the feeder it went through a sieve with holes as big as an old sixpence and came through a slit known as a mouth onto greased trays. There it was cut into lengths to fit these trays. Any offcuts that overlapped the trays were quickly cut off by another girl, rolled onto her lap and returned to the feeder. The cutting job was usually reserved for any girl that was pregnant as this was a sitting-down job.

As the liquorice went along the conveyor belt the tins were taken off by two girl stackers, one at each side. One girl turned the tin towards the other who held it with her to be stacked in two rows as high as six feet. Little legs between the tins prevented the liquorice from sticking to the trays underneath. When the trays reached about six feet high, which was as high as the women could reach, another woman would come with a trolley jack and wheel them precariously into an oven. One woman's job was to constantly go along the four machines and remove all the stacked pallets for the oven.

The oven would hold about ten platforms of liquorice at any one time so the woman would wait until the oven was full before closing the doors and setting the timer for it to cook. It had to be cooked at a specific temperature so that it would not burn.

If you're good looking the lads want to help you

■ I was only at Wilkinson's for six months because I got pregnant. Even when they knew I was carrying they still had me packing great big trays. They liked their pound of flesh.

■ When they introduced baby allsorts I used to get sick of the smell of them. My back used to ache with all the bending over. It was three o'clock some days before I straightened my back.

■ When I first started I used to shift a 56 pound bag of sugar and four buckets of hot water on a pair of wheels. There was that much dust we were like little snowmen. Our eyelashes were white with it.

■ I've worked at Dunhill's, now Haribo, for seven months and I work in the NID. They have NID one, two, three and four. NID is the name of the Dutch machines. It's all men in the NID room. Women work in the Yanato room. Yanato is the name of the machine in that room.

I work on shifts and make jelly products with a team of five. We do morning and afternoon shifts alternately with two teams. We process sweets going through the machine, where they get weighed, sorted, put into stoves to harden and then taken for packing. There is a main operator on the machine who puts colours and flavours in. Then there's one of us at the front and one at the back putting sweets in and taking them off. Another takes them off for packing and a kitchen man checks the temperature. We all work together and change round so that we don't get bored. The supervisor will muck in and help and is there to make sure everything's going alright. Some rooms have a team leader who is Grade I, and training to be a supervisor. They have a grading system from 1 to 4 your number depends on what jobs you can do. Grade I means you can do all the jobs and can go on to be a supervisor.

I've been told the conditions are a lot stricter since Haribo took over. Lads have said that a few years ago you could eat your snap at your machine, now you have to go to the canteen. Hygiene standards are very high now because the company are going for the British Standard which means goods are of the highest quality and so can compete on the market.

■ One of my friends had to go in the NID room on the drum. Sometimes we go in to help the lads when they are short. You work on a big metal churn where jelly babies are waxed. The jelly babies come off the machine, go into the drum, then you take them out and stack them on trays of eighteen at a time.

She didn't like working in there because the lads tend to have you on a bit. It's like this. If you're good looking the lads will help you because its quite a hard, hot and heavy job. If you're a bit plain, though, the lads take the mickey and leave you to get on with it.

■ I had moved back to Pontefract from North Devon. I got myself a

35

If you're good looking the lads want to help you

job at Wilkinson's liquorice works to tide me over. I had seen the advert for workers in the paper and went for an interview but I didn't really take to the work, I suppose I'm not cut out to working in a factory.

I started on the five till nine afternoon shift and I can remember having to wear a silly net mop cap. I was put on a conveyor belt sorting party packs, then shifted to a room where bubbly gum was made. I ended up making a right mess of the job in this room. The supervisor showed me a steel funnel with a table underneath with boxes on it. Apparently one of the girls took pallets of bubbly gum and emptied them into the funnel where they were counted and sent down into the boxes these have to be made up quickly and packaged with the bubbly gum.

Well, it was a nightmare. All these bubblies, about 500 of them, came firing down this funnel while I was desperately trying to make my box. They went everywhere, over my knees and all over the floor, so they put me on pouring the bubblies into the funnel. Again I missed the funnel and chucked bubblies everywhere.

The supervisor could see I was a bit upset so she put me on another job. I stayed a few months, the money was quite good but I couldn't work in a factory for good, it's too boring doing the same thing over and over again.

■ In the liquorice factory there were some terrible jobs, one of these was glazing the liquorice. Sticks of hard juice would be dipped into a glaze and then carried on wire trays into the stove rooms to dry. The women would get the glaze all over them. They wore larding aprons' made from washed sugar bags to keep the front of their overalls clean but they still ended up with the glaze all over. They usually went home with their hands stained brown.

■ My friend's sister was feeding paste into the refiner when the machine set off before she had her arm clear. It was nearly severed. The doctors managed to save it though and she received £100 compensation.

■ I worked for ten years in the old factory until it closed, then

I wore my wedding ring out with a shovel

transferred to the new factory. I worked on a Toffee Crisp wrapping machine, taking mini Toffee Crisps off a belt, feeding them into a machine which wraps them. I had been in the new factory about six months when there was a vacancy for a shop steward on the After Eight department. My name was put forward and I got it.

Sometimes it is very frustrating but other times, when you can help someone get time off because of a sick child or an ageing parent that needs looking after, it can be very rewarding. Of course, if a good pay deal is awarded you are everyone's friend. A shop steward is more of a listening ear or a social worker than the militant political worker that the papers make union people out to be. I like fair play for everyone, not just the ones whose faces fit.

■ Some sweet factory foremen can be real clever. I was working in a storeroom as an electrician and had to hang up a very heavy armoured cable along the ceiling. Right where we wanted to set up our steps was a big pile of brand new tin boxes, shaped like a book. Each box had a tiny lock and a fancy picture on the front. The boxes were for a new line of sweets which were for sale at Christmas. I asked this snotty foreman to move these boxes three times but nothing happened. My boss didn't like to see us doing nothing so we decided to carry on. We climbed onto the pile and began to lift the heavy cable. Naturally in no time at all we had damaged quite a number of these boxes. Eventually word got to the foreman. Then a man soon came with a fork lift to shift the lot.

I wore my wedding ring out with a shovel

■ We used to all sing together. One song I remember well is *Now is the Hour*. The cream room and cutting room all joined in. We used to ask if there were any pallets to take back to other rooms or any excuse just to get a change of sweet. There was the gum room, a pan room that made sugared almonds and the cake room. In the early days we never had a full day's work so we had to clean windows and clean all the dirty corners out. We also went on other jobs if we had no work .

We didn't have a canteen when I first went to Dunhill's, we had to

39

sit and eat our sandwiches where we worked with liquorice allsorts for afters. It was hard work standing on a box to mix the liquorice allsorts on a table with a shovel. I wore my wedding ring out with that shovel.

We had a good forewoman called Elsie; she would send someone to fetch the smokers from the toilet if they stayed too long but she wasn't a bad 'un.

■ The department near to the boiler house would be continually working, running out liquorice sheets which, along with cream sheeting, would form blocks from which liquorice allsorts would be cut. The lasses in this room were the hardest worked in the factory.

Liquorice sheets ran onto eight foot by sixteen inch greased boards where a girl would cut off measured lengths of the hot paste, pick it up with her free hand and toss it to the hopper. Each one then had to pick up the board with the sheet of liquorice and quickly stack it on a steel rack. As the rack filled up it took longer to get back to the table. There were usually two or three girls in there and the heat from the stoves was unbearable. The ventilation was very poor which didn't help matters. At about two thirty, the supply of paste ran out but their job wasn't over. Then they had to start cleaning everything, the boards, the tins, the machines and hand scrub the floor. The floors were white with scrubbing.

■ One day I went to work in the spanish room. Dipping licks was my job that day. Licks was our name for the hard spanish you dipped in sherbert. My job was to dip the licks into a black shiny liquid to finish them off. We had a basket like a chip frying basket only bigger. The licks were put into the basket, dipped into the liquid, drained by shaking and spread onto wire racks. Before we started we tore neck and arm holes into green plastic sacks and wore them to keep us clean.

I was busily working, getting mucky, with black stuff all over the green sack, when there was a loud ringing. It was the fire alarm. Did I feel a burk, filing out into Queen Street with my green sack on, covered with black streaks. They could have warned me. It was only a practice.

■ Women wore a smock and a turban, but were not allowed to wear hair clips or earrings in case they fell in the spanish. Only wedding rings were allowed, which was as well really, as any other type would have been caked-up with liquorice.

Anyone needing to go to the toilet had to wait until someone could look after their machine. Occasionally a conveyor belt would break and all the women would rush to the toilet. Other times women would take advantage of the machines running short of liquorice and go as well.

Tea-break was ten minutes long then a woman came into the cutting room with a trolley and a geyser. Cheap tea and biscuits were sold. The young girls in the cutting room would sometimes make a little figure out of spanish and put it on the side of the trays. When work was resumed after tea break you would hear a roar of laughter at the other end of the room as that tray went through the system to the next girls. These figures were never put into the oven but always put back into the feeder. The work was hard, and hot, with no windows, you felt closed in and overpowered in summer. The hours were from eight to five Monday to Friday, eight to twelve on a Saturday. There was one week's holiday per year and the wage was about £4 a week.

In those days it cost 16/- to have your photo taken at Maud's Photographers. Sixteen girls got together and paid 1/- each week to put their name in a box; the names were drawn out and the first one had her photo taken first and so on, until every girl had got a photo.

■ The upper gum room had a side door that led onto the railway lines. One day Castleford Rugby League Team were playing the touring side at Wheldon Road. Jack, the boss on my bay, got his pipe and said, "I shan't be long. I'm just going down the lines to see what the score is, if I'm not back in twenty minutes put a wetting on." By the time he got back the torps were ready for coming out. He'd stopped for the whole match.

Maisie and Miriam worked on Edgar's bay. Edgar was on holiday and Mick was running his own bay as well as Edgar's. Maisie and Miriam took their shoes off, left them under the pan and went for a walk round. Mick kept glancing under the pans as he walked up and down his bay. He thought they were still there working but all he saw was two pairs of empty shoes.

41

Better than the men

When I worked in the bake room there were four characters there, Ivy, Joyce, Edie and Big Doreen. The headwear had changed from the turban to white caps with elastic round the front. They used to pull the cap down right over their eyes, take their teeth out, put a spanish pipe in their mouth, screw their faces up just like Popeye and sing all the old songs.

The job I have now is completely different. I work on the Toffee Crisp wrapping machines, Chocolates come down the belt fifteen in a row and, as they pass you, you take all fifteen with a square scoop and feed them on to the infeed belt. As the chocolates go into the machine you automatically keep it filled and when the reel is empty you just thread another reel on. The job is a lot easier but it is not the same, no singing, no acting about. I don't believe in where there's muck there's money but I do believe in the good old days.

I'd go back in the Bellamy factory tomorrow, hoss work or not.

Better than any man

■ I started working at Dunhill's/Haribo about five years ago. I've worked there on and off since. It's Haribo now but most of us still call it Dunhill's.

I work in the packing room. You're not supposed to talk or have a laugh, you're supposed to just get on with the job. You get some that will have a laugh and some that are obsessed with the job, like this lass who works on my machine. She's the machine operator and likes you to know that she's in charge, likes to tell you what to do. She gets on at me but I know the job anyway. This particular day, though, she was running about and getting in a flap with the work and she ran straight over my feet with a trolley 20lb full of Tesco Twists, and nearly broke all my toes. She didn't even notice she'd done it. I felt so sick I couldn't speak.

■ Anne Lowe, she knew them machines inside out, better than any fitter. She had to unjam a machine once, as Dave wasn't there. She fell and was all over that machine. What a sight. Big Betty was holding her legs up in the air so she wouldn't fall into the thing and Anne was shouting, "Don't let me go Betty!"

■ There were two liquorice boiling rooms, one in the old building, near the boiler house, and one in the new building near the Knottingley Road entrance. These boiling rooms had to have an early paste ready for the early shift to start work at seven thirty. When the mix had completed its cycle it had to be shovelled out with an aluminium shovel into strong aluminium trays. The sweat off the man with the shovel had to be seen to be believed. Each tray would probably weigh about 56lbs and six or eight of these would eventually be manhandled onto wooden platforms. A Slingsby trolley would then be used to transport the mix to wherever it was needed.

■ I enjoyed my time working at Ewbank's liquorice works in Pontefract. My job was to strip Pontefract cakes from boards onto a belt ready for packing. When everybody asked what occupation I had, my boyfriend used to delight in saying, "Oh, she's got a right job; she's a stripper."

■ I worked the twilight shift at Wilkinson's, half past four while nine at night in the cream room. In this room layers of cream and spanish were put together for liquorice allsorts then put into the machine to be chopped into small squares. I used to sort out the mis-shapes coming out of the machine.

■ I liked eating sweets when I first started work at the liquorice works and I ate quite a lot, but I started to put on weight so I had to try not to eat so many. I was crying one evening at home with toothache when my dad said, "It just serves you right. You shouldn't eat so many of those bloody spice at the factory."

After you have worked there a while you don't eat so many; you get fed up with them. But if ever I could get to the mushroom department I would eat, I love mushrooms when they are still fresh and a stick of spanish just made is lovely.

■ Mr Wilkinson was in charge of the almond room. The workers were always told Mr Wilkinson took the secret of making sugar almonds to Dunhill's. He had three sons and one daughter working with him there.

■ We sent sweets all over the world. I remember once getting an order from Canada, Winnipeg in fact. I had to enter the order in my ledger and then tell them on the machine what was required and what day it had to be on its way. This order was for two tons of jelly babies, maple coloured. I then had to pack them all and load them onto the wagon for the journey across the world.

■ The fashion for sweets and confectionery now is NCFs or *natural colours and flavours*. We get quite a lot of orders for sweets with them in. In Arabia they like Pear flavour, and the French like children's mix and that has to be all natural. Mind you we still do a lot of the ordinary as well.

■ Wilkinson's sweets went to all parts of the world. There was a large despatch area. To send sweets abroad special boxes were made of wood and lined with metal. Sometimes just after Christmas it would be a bit quiet then Walker would say, "When oranges are in there's a few less sweets sold."

■ When I went on staff I was in the Personnel Department, setting on new workers, but they told me that when the new factory was built, I was to be moved as they had someone with better qualifications than me. Some interviewers would not set on people with better qualifications than themselves as they thought they might be after their jobs. The highlight of my career was when I went into production and I was sent to be in charge of factory work with Maureen Firth.

■ I once loaded a van all on my own. There were 5,000 boxes each holding six smaller boxes of liquorice allsorts. When the wagon was full I had nothing to do so Mr Hargreaves came over and handed me a pair

45

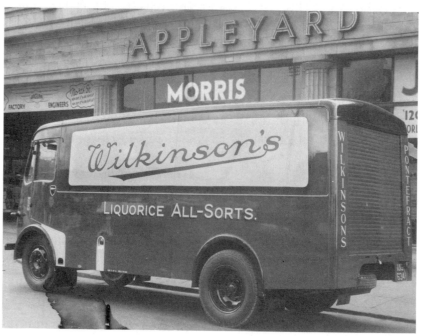

We deliver anywhere

of scissors. "Here," he said, "go and help her with that there spanish." The job was cutting up strips of spanish.

■ One day this young girl came to me and said," I've a confession to make. I asked the boss not to send me with you as I thought you were a clever bugger."
" Why did you think that?" I asked.
"Well it was the way you walked," she replied.

■ This fellow was leaning on the back of a machine, a right shirker, he was. Well, he fell asleep and one of the bosses was talking away to him as he stood there, now fast asleep. If the boss hadn't tapped him on the shoulder he'd have still been snoring away. The boss hadn't noticed he was asleep and as he tapped him, he said, "Are you listening to me?"
"Yes." said the bloke with a start.
"Well get on with what I told you then," said the boss as he walked away.

■ You have to get under a machine to clean the starch out. Well, old Don is a bit chubby and one day he went under the machine and got fast. His belt got caught so he was stuck good and proper and couldn't move. Well, you know what the lads are like, they were acting about and lobbing sweets at him. Finally they had to get a fitter to take off the side panels to get him out. They cut his belt and pulled him out by his legs.

■ I've heard of sneaking out of work but this kid got caught sneaking in. He was climbing over the fence when he got copped. He told the boss that some kids had kidnapped him and left him in Castleford. You see you're not supposed to come into work late.

■ I think the lads have more of a laugh than we do, they seem to get away with more than the lasses. At the Christmas do in the Wilton Ballroom, Castleford, women are after men, not the other way round. The management give give you £10 and some free beer or a Martini or something like that. You also get four bottles of wine on the day you

47

break up for Christmas. If you get married and you both work there, the management gives you £50.

■ I worked at Dunhill's from the age of fourteen until I got married. My husband married me to get me away from Dunhill's because it was so awful. I earned 12/- a week and went home for my lunch every day on my bike. The dinner dance was held on a Friday night so all the workers were allowed Saturday morning off, without pay, if they wanted it. At the dance everybody used to sing to the owner. *For he's a jolly good fellow.* I used to sing, "For he's a bloody old dog."
It was slave labour! Mr Fobs, owner of Dunhill's, built some almshouses for the old people.

■ I am a five pack packer. I take five After Eight mints and a complaints ticket and put them in a five pack box and close the lid down tight. The box then goes onto a conveyor belt on its way to its next phase. This is the machine which covers the box with cellophane paper. It then goes through some heated rollers which seals all the loose ends.

■ The wooden boxes Wilkinson's used mainly for export orders were made on the premises by four ladies - Mary Frain, Annie Adams, Annie Price and Mary Bloy.

■ I was on a YTS scheme, training to work in a shop. I left school in March and did that till June. I went to the Chamber of Commerce in Pontefract for a month and I ended up here in September. I'm working in the mushroom room at the moment. It's like a production line. You start by sieving the coconut and then it's levelled out onto trays. Then it goes onto a machine that puts 325 hollows into the coconut. I know it's 325 because you've got to learn that. They ask you at the end of the week. After the hollows have been made a woman tips in a mixture of gelatin and cocoa powder. Then the stalks are put in by some women. That's all done by hand still. They get them between their thumb and first finger to place them. They can't half go fast. All the coconut that isn't used goes round again for the next lot.

■ Another awful job at the liquorice factory was washing the boards. The liquorice cream would stick to the boards and was scraped off from time to time but when they got really bad they had to be soaked and scrubbed. If you ran out of work you sometimes were sent to help with this, it was a terrible job. When the boards got broken you took them down to the boiler house and they were put into the boiler fire. I liked to go down there, as it was near to the extract boiling pan and Mr Jordan would sometimes give you a lump off the black liquorice extract.

■ The hardest job was taking the spanish off a machine on boards into the hot stove room. It was so hot that all we would wear would be bra and pants underneath our overalls. It was like being in a bloody sauna all day long.

■ "If you can't see that owl on that gate throw them out!" That's what they used to say. You see, one of the seals on the Pontefract Cakes was a gate with an owl on it. The checkers wanted to see everything in detail.

Sweet anticipation

....AND ALL THINGS NICE

A carnival of colour

■ A red brick floor smothered by a mulch of metal trays is swarming with every child's delight - spice. There is a riot of colour, shapes and sizes; sunshine yellow, orange, red, lime green, pink, and purple. Plastic trays, heavy with sugary loads, criss-cross in a torpedo sandwich. Footprints walk in sweet white dust on the floor. Burnt toffee, like sludge, swamps plastic baths like fat mud pies that any kid would revel in. Pontefract cakes dot conveyor belts like black rubber buttons and a giant machine lets out a monotonous hiss every six seconds. The smell of lime and liquorice climbs the pink painted walls and lingers in the air to freshen the senses and trigger the taste buds. Desiccated coconut crowns chocolate covered mushrooms, while the pop group, Oceanic, go dream tripping through the loud speaker system. Tubs of icing sugar stand in groups like crinoline ladies waiting for the next waltz while real ladies empty jellies into six orbiting barrels. The cyclone of colour and scent of lime jellies make the senses forget it's winter. Women, uniformed in white caps and pinnies, some with blue rubber gloves and much needed earplugs, are busy lifting, emptying, packing and stacking, but they still find time to help one another and laugh; team work, team spirit. The redundant old Avery scales watch from a far wall, as perhaps does the ghost of an old monk from the days when the building was a monastery. The grounds of the factory were at one time a liquorice field. The monks used to dig it up for their own medicinal use. All that is left of the fields now is a circle of canes. The liquorice we use is imported these days. Wilkinson's is a carnival now; a carnival of colour, music and laughter.

■ I wouldn't like to say that Dunhill's and Wilkinson's are in competition with one another, but their stuff doesn't look half as nice as ours. I'm not saying that their coca-cola bottles don't look as nice as ours but their mushrooms look awful.

■ Squirrel Confectioners at Stockport had a very good reputation for sugared almonds but standards were higher for everything at Wilkinson's. I used to think that we made a better liquorice allsort than Bassett's. It's funny that Bassett's should buy us out.

I used to go to Monkhill station and there would be stuff piled up ready to go back to a certain factory I won't mention. The station porter would say, "That's another lot going back."

These days mixtures are computerised, they no longer have to depend on the taste buds of a person so there should be no excuse for the stuff tasting rough.

■ At the beginning of the year one of my first jobs was braying the mats. I used to come home muckier than I did when I worked at the pit. Other days I'd be creosoting fences, or weeding the garden. I could do that stripped to the waist in the summer, it was lovely. In some ways it was that variety that kept me at the factory. It wasn't monotonous then, I wasn't like somebody on a conveyor belt.

■ Working in despatch gives you a good bearing. I have educated myself in geography through working in that department. If you were to say to me, Devizes, I should come back with Wiltshire. We sent stuff all over from Wilkinson's. We used to export to places as far away as Kuala Lumpur. We'd a lot of traffic to Copenhagen and Malmo and a very good traffic to Holland and New York. Paul Spitz, a Jewish chap used to come to the factory now and again. He was an agent for overseas orders.

■ Sweets were despatched all over the world from Wilkinson's. During the war a consignment was sent out to the soldiers serving abroad and some of us were asked to put in our names and addresses. Not long after, I received a letter from a soldier serving in Sudan and I wrote back sending a photo. After a while I had to stop writing as he was getting a bit too friendly. He would say he was madly in love with me. I had a boyfriend and it didn't go down very well when he found out.

■ As a child I used to love to be around Wilkinson's front gate when the workers were coming out after a day's work. Some of the workers would run down the driveway, others would be on bikes and there would be a dash to the two bus stops outside the gate.

You could tell by their overalls what job they did in the factory. If the khaki overall was clean they most likely worked in the packing room. If they were covered in a white powder it meant that they worked in the cream department and a brown stain on the front of their overalls meant they worked in the spanish room or the glazing department.

■ You wear your hat like a status symbol now. There's a blue hat to say you're training, and a bottle green hat for the next stage and after that you get a white one. Everybody hates the bottle green hat so they try to get off that as quick as they can. Can you imagine anybody wearing a bottle green hat? It's like being in bloody judo trying for your different belts.

■ Mr Frank Archer's office was just a large wardrobe situated in the corner of the cream mixing room. There he had a large wooden barrel for doing his paper work on. Each year we had to tell him when we'd reached another birthday and he passed the information to the office so we would receive our appropriate rise in pay. He used to interview people for any vacancies that came up and we also went to him if we wished to resign. When we left school at 14 years old we all had to find our own jobs as there were no Job Centres in those days.

■ Mr Walter Marshall was one of the big business men behind the firm. Hearsay was that he had gambled a lot of money on the Kentucky Derby and came up. He died the week I should have started so they knocked me back a week. They say he used to want to see every single worker who started at the company.

■ Mr Sharp was the manager before Mr Harrison. I'll never forget one incident between them. Mr Harrison tripped up and he was scrabbling about with his hands trying to keep his face off the floor. Mr Sharp

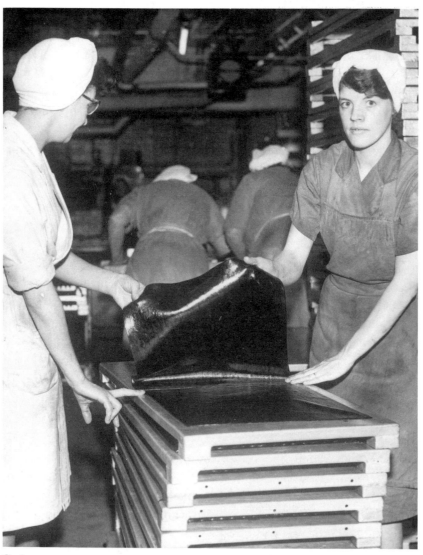

Strippers

turned round and with a look of complete disdain said, "Norman whatever are you doing you frightful little thing?" He was a stickler was Mr Sharp. The first thing he used to do when he walked into a place was kick the dustbin over to see if anybody was hiding anything.

■ I think people have better opportunities for work these days. Years ago in the Fifties, when I left school, if you were a lass you had to go to work and earn money, usually in one of the local factories. Those working in the shops thought they were better than the factory workers. A friend of mine, Enid, got going out with this lad but his mother didn't think she was good enough because she worked in a factory. The lad only worked at the pit. Some looked down on factory work but a lot worked there.

■ Mrs Siddall was well built and was super fit. She marched the length of the factory like a sergeant. She ended up being nicknamed "Pizzey" because when we saw her coming we used to go "Psst, pssst." She'd be on top of you before you realised, she was that fit.

■ I worked in a shop where the pay wasn't so good so I decided to go to the liquorice works to earn more money. The work wasn't bad but I couldn't come to terms with the atmosphere amongst the women who worked there. Swearing was all around you, some of the women used terrible language. I wasn't a snob but I wasn't used to that. Sex was always a topic of conversation. One day a woman, feeling behind my ears said, "I can tell by the lumps behind your ears that you had a sexy night last night." She couldn't have been further from the truth, but I steered clear of her after that.

■ In the old days everyone knew everyone else. Now our names are sewn on our overalls. They say it's more friendly to be able to talk to someone and say their name. It was a lot more friendly when you bothered to find out what people were called and not just reading the name off an overall as people do today.

- We were all mates together. One person's troubles belonged to all of us, likewise we all shared anyone's joy. Any quarrels were quickly sorted out, we didn't believe in holding grudges; life was too short and we all went to work for the same thing - money. It was just as easy to be pleasant with each other as to fall out.

Hey up! Archer's coming

- My first job when leaving school was at Ewbank's Liquorice Works in the spanish room. My wage was £7 a week working from 7.30 to 5.30. I then went to work at Wilkinson's in the mushroom department. One day I had a tiff with the forewoman and we got to blows. I had to face the manager and got six weeks' suspension. I took my case to a tribunal and won it. I got my six weeks' wages backdated to me and was offered my job back but I refused and left.

My next job was at Dunhill's where I worked in the fan room. We had to wear clogs because the floor was so slippy. The most enjoyable part about Dunhill's was attending for the Miss Candy Queen Contest, at Wordsworths' Ballroom and Pontefract Town Hall. I finished second in both contests, and was then invited to take part in the all-finals contest in Leeds. I was very unlucky and finished second again. The audience was not very pleased with the verdict and they showed it. It turned out that one of the works managers of the girl that won it was a panel judge. Mind there were no sour grapes on my part as the girl who won was lovely.

- The secretary of Wilkinson's got me my job. His name was Albert Cook and he used to come to our house to see my mother before choir practice. I was fifteen, with strong leanings towards the navy, and had already got a place at Chatham as a boy sailor.

"I know you want to go, but there might be a vacancy on transport," Mr Cook said. I was interested but I wanted to know how much they would pay me. "Ten bob" was the response.

"Nay I'm getting 21/6d down the pit. I can't take less than that." I replied.

Mother said, "Be satisfied."

In those days it seemed as though Mother's whole motive in life was to be satisfied. So I had to be satisfied.

■ I left Wilkinson's because when I was six months gone and I could get my full benefit. I was luckier than a lot because I didn't get morning sickness. You used to see a lot of them running to the lavatory on a morning when they saw all the different mixtures and could hear everybody whispering then, "I bet she's expecting." I was glad by the time I left because I'd got right big.

■ Father gave me 2/6d out of my wage of 12/5d. I had to buy clothes off it. In those days we got two breaks during the day; ten minutes in the morning and the same in the afternoon. There was no music played through the factory when I was there. In fact there wasn't any heating let alone music. You even had to ask permission to go to the toilet. They used to spy on us, sneak around trying to catch us having a laugh. But we had a system. Whoever was keeping an eye out would shout "Hey up, Archer's coming!" We used to talk about the dancing and our boyfriends. In the rolling out room where the big brass rollers flattened the liquorice and cream, they used to sing *Wedding Bells Are Ringing For You*. If he heard us Mr Archer would scream at us to stop taking liberties. They didn't like us having fun in the factory but on the other hand they had tennis courts and me and Charlie used to play tennis. I got married in 1940 and I've never been near the place since, I wouldn't go back under the same conditions.

■ One Saturday morning Pam and I were on the tug lifts, bringing finished sweets out of the stoves and taking sweets that had just been made back into the stoves. We went into the gum room early, before anyone else started work, to make some room in the stoves for the new sweets. I was pulling the tug lift, which meant I was facing the stack and had to keep looking over my shoulder to make sure I didn't bump into anything. Pam was at the back of the stack pushing it.

I was coming out of the stoves into the gum room when I glanced over

57

my shoulder and saw someone. I shouted, "Pam, stop pushing!" Her head appeared from behind the stack.

"Why?" she said.

"I don't want to knock the poor bugger down, do I?" I replied.

"There's no bugger there," she said.

I looked over my shoulder and, sure enough, the room was empty.

"Who the 'ell were you going to bump into?" she said.

"The tall bloke, long black jacket, winged collar shirt, no white coat on."

"Oh bloody 'ell!" we both said together.

We each ran to the two doors that led into the gum room. There was no-one there and no time for anyone to get out of the next rooms. We'd seen the ghost. He was seen quite often in Bellamy's, always dressed in old- fashioned clothes. Women in the gum room would often jump and yell out. Someone, unseen, had pinched their bum.

■ The Germans took over while I worked there, they enforced more efficiency. They put me on a vibrator, I've been on it 12 years this year, I enjoy the work.

■ Joan Bray was the factory welder. She used to wear proper overalls and welding goggles. She's retired now. There weren't many men here at one time and I think it was a better atmosphere. Edie Whitworth used to charge up and down a bit, but she was always fair.

■ Edie never swore at home; her husband thought she never swore but in the factory every second word was a four letter one. We used to say she must have slipped.

■ I started working at Dunhill's when I left school at fifteen. I was always in trouble for talking and I didn't like having to stand at a machine all day. The older women were always on to you to go faster, but they had been there years. At fifteen you soon get upset but I suppose you get used to it.

58

■ Nobody could have worked harder than the women who carried the liquorice boards into the drying ovens. They were lathered all day long, wet through and just wore smocks over their knickers.

■ I get a laugh with other women, I like to talk. Once when I was talking to the secretary she looked mesmerised and I said, "I know, I can talk a glass eye to sleep."

■ One day we'd knocked off early for some holiday or other. I found some men's overalls, got into them in a fashion and I shouted, "Where are they all, they should be working." The lasses faces were a picture. They all came rushing out to do some work then someone recognised me. I was called some names but it was a good laugh.

■ The most exciting time was the fancy dress competition. It was the annual Christmas dance and Mr Baxter said there would be fancy dress and asked for volunteers to advertise liquorice. Our Alice was right full of ideas. She said to Mr Baxter, "My sister will do it if you agree. I'll get her up as a Hawaiian girl." Mr Baxter said alright so Alice got started. She made a hula hula skirt out of spanish, all braids attached to a belt and sewed by machine. Alice said,
"What about the top?" We didn't know what to do.
"I know," said Alice, "I'll make it out of a plug, glazed pieces of spanish. I'll cut a butterfly shape out."
"I'm not wearing that next to me skin, Al. When I get warm it'll all stick."
"All right then, fusspot. Get a pair of old gym knickers, navy ones. I'll cut a piece off them to the same shape and you can put that underneath. It'll give you a bit of padding anyway."
So the bodice was made of plug. It had Wilkinson's Plug stamped in medallions all over it! We made earrings out of plug too and fastened them with cotton hung over my ears. Then we used sherbet dabs for round my neck.
"I don't want any round me ankles, Al."
"You do, You do! Get on! Leave it to me."

59

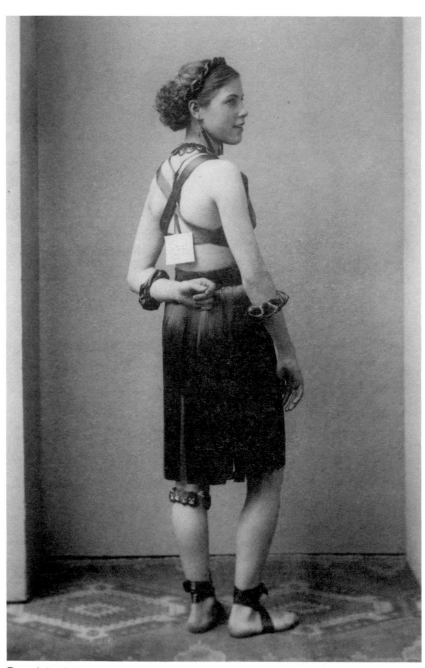

Spanish girl

I wanted slippers or sandals on my feet but Alice wouldn't have that. "You'll take the effect away altogether."

I had to have my hair all fuzzy wuzzy, Alice did it with mam's old curling tongs. Then she stood back to look at me.

"There's summat missing."

"I can't see what," said mam, "there's no room to hang any more on her."

"I know what it is! Get the cocoa tin out, mam, she's got to be a dusky maid."

The competition was held in Pontefract Town Hall. I were right nervous. Alice had me practising the walk.

"When you come on, get your hand on your hip and sway your hips like this. And smile for heaven's sake. Look like a winner, don't look so glum." I were terrified, lips clenched.

We walked round the dance floor several times so everyone could get a view. I wouldn't have liked to have all boxes on, that was what most of the other fancy dress girls had. Everytime I walked past the balcony, a shout went up, "Yes! Yes!" All my friends were yelling and clapping. Eventually the judge got up.

"We'll have Miss Skidmore because she was the most original and the best dressed." We did laugh after that, best dressed. Truth was I hadn't much on!

The prize was a right big basket with each of Heinz's 57 varieties; my mam had that, and a green trinket set from Bagley's, our Alice had that. It was all buzzing and chatting in the hall because I'd won.

All the young lads started grabbing the strands off my skirt and eating them. I'd only about five or six braids on as I came down the Town Hall steps. It was just as well I'd black knickers on! The boss was a bit put out with that and said I shouldn't have let the lads do it. How could I have stopped them, I'd like to know!

Three weeks later Mr Baxter got me to put the costume on again to go and have a photo taken at Maud's. Alice had to get a whole lot more braid to replace the bits of skirt that had been eaten!

■ There were starch bins in the gum room where we emptied new sacks

61

of starch, they were about six feet long and three feet wide. When it was someone's birthday they were grabbed by their arms and legs and thrown into the starch bin. They crawled about covered in starch like zombies. It got everywhere, eyes, nose, mouth, in your bra, in your knickers, everywhere.

■ There was once an argument between two spinster sisters and another woman who complained about the non-pareils they were making and having to neglect. The sisters were thoroughly sick of her sharp tongue so one of them picked up a box of starch and threw it all over her. She muttered, walked off and never complained again!

On another occasion, the room where they blew the starch off the jelly babies ended up looking like a thick fog, and everyone went home looking like snowmen. I had to vacuum my hair to get it out. I later found out that the fitter had put the nozzle on the machine the wrong way, so it was blowing all the starch out instead of sucking it in.

■ I got very hot in the factory and the best part was breaking out. Rose said to me, "Fancy a glass of beer?"

"I would but how do we get out?"

"Leave it to me," she said. So off she went to see the forewoman.

"Winnie, I have to go to the dentist to have a tooth out at one thirty but I can't go on my own as I always faint so can I take my mate with me?"

Winnie very reluctantly said, "Alright then, bugger off, but don't be long." So off we went at one thirty as far as the Gardeners' Arms. After a quick look round to see if anybody was watching in we went.

Rose had to go to the dentist more times than anyone in the factory. She dreaded Winnie looking in her mouth. She hadn't a tooth missing.

■ I saved my pocket money and bought myself a bike. It was only a second hand one and it was worth a lot more than the £5 I paid but a neighbour let me have it for just that.

Getting to the liquorice works then was a doddle. I really enjoyed riding my bike early on a morning and could be at work in ten minutes.

The bike shed at Wilkinson's was always full of bikes and you could leave your bike there without fear of anyone pinching it.

One morning I had the fright of my life. Freewheeling down Baghill Lane, my brakes failed at the bottom and I went sailing out onto the main Knottingley Road. Lucky for me there was no traffic coming at the time, only one parked car. The owner called out to me, "You stupid little bugger!" I made sure my bike had new brake blocks after that.

Vera Lynn pops in

■ Visitors were often brought round Wilkinson's. I can remember Vera Lynn visiting with her husband. She stopped by me and asked if I enjoyed my work. I had to say yes as the boss was with her.

Norman Evans also came round one day, I asked for his autograph and he obliged by drawing me his favourite *over the garden wall* sketch.

■ Amy Marshall, that was the Marshall's daughter, married Noel Gay. They talk about him on television now.

■ Clegg came to Wilkinson's once. You'll know him, he talks right funny. They call the programme, *Clegg's People,* it's on after *Calendar.* They wanted to show folk how they did hand stamping on the Ponty cakes years since. The only thing was they couldn't find our stamp anywhere. In the end they had to send down to the museum for one.

■ One of the nice things about the old days was *Workers' Playtime* . At break times in the canteen the radio would be on and we'd listen to a live broadcast from a work's canteen somewhere. There would be a singer, a comedian and maybe a ventriloquist, all in half an hour. Many now famous stars started on this programme; Frankie Howard, Ann Shelton and many others.

There wasn't a canteen of any kind in 1924 but a lady from one of the rows of houses situated in Dunhills' yard was kind enough to make tea and hand it up at dinner times to those who couldn't get home.

Workers playtime

■ I can remember a gentleman who was secretary to the firm at Wilkinson's. He was also a prominent figure in the Methodist chapel at Featherstone, playing the organ for the choir. His name was Mr Albert Cook and he was very respected by everyone at Wilkinson's, especially some of us he taught to sing after work in the canteen. He formed a choir and would teach us songs like *Barbara Allan* and *Danny Boy*. There weren't many of us in the choir but we all enjoyed it.

■ We never had any music on. For one thing if you worked in the pan room you couldn't hear yourself speak and for another you weren't allowed to speak. You had to ask permission to go to the toilet. It was worse than being at school. I remember the lasses in the rolling room getting a bit carried away now and again. If anybody was getting wed they'd sing *Wedding Bells Are Ringing* and they'd knock their rolling pins together like a bell.

■ The boss, Jimmy Ellis, played the trumpet for the Salvation Army. I called him Eddy Calvert .We would sing songs in the cake room for the bosses. Cath Keers' song was *I'll take you home again Kathleen*.

■ One Friday night the lasses in the gum room were going out together because Sharon was getting married and it was her hen party. We went to the Bier Keller in Leeds and, oh! how the lager flowed. Later on we went to a nightclub. We had all bought green felt hats at the Bier Keller and were wearing them on the way home in the bus, all apart from one lass who was suddenly very ill into hers.

The bus dropped us each off at our homes. One young lass of 18 had been locked out of the house by her parents as she was home late. It was a nice summer evening so she got a garden chair from the shed and fell asleep in it in the garden. Poor lass, there was a very heavy dew that morning and when she woke up the dye from her green hat had trickled down her face. It took nigh on a week for it to completely wear off her face. Looking back we had some great nights out.

■ I used to have some right good mates in the factory, we had some great laughs. At Christmas, when we got our double money, a gang of us went to the Railway pub and got legless, then spent the rest of the day in the bog being sick. Bellamy's workers went to the Garden House, then spilled over to the Miners Arms.

■ On race days women and children stood or squatted on the route from the park gates to the race course with tins of cakes, chanting "Pontefract cakes 3d and 4d a tin," hoping to sell to the race goers as they arrived on foot from Tanshelf station.

■ Mr Godson was very good at Christmas. He paid for a seven course dinner at the Assembly Rooms for all the workers. This was followed by a dance which went on until two o'clock in the morning.

For a few weeks before Christmas the sweets were packed in fancy tins. They were that nice that the lasses used to buy them for Christmas presents. There would be two pounds in weight in these tins and they cost about 1/6d. Some had Laughing Cavaliers on and some had swans.

■ I remember the first works dance when everyone was buying new dresses. The owners, Mr Geoff Godson and Mr Ken Godson, always mixed with everyone at these dances. Mr Godson moved from Wilkinson's to Dunhill's and he persuaded some Wilkinson's workers to go with him. There he formed a cricket team for the men.

■ There were tennis courts at the side of Wilkinson's. Tennis was one of the things that made going to work worthwhile because it was flaming awful otherwise. Every year the workers played the owners at a game, the workers always won of course.

■ At Dunhill's they had a hockey team. I played for two winters before I left. I remember scoring a goal against Painton and Baldwin, that was a wool factory in Wakefield. We played up at the top of the Rookeries.

■ When Wilkies had their centenary they gave us a Spode plate apiece.

They were all individually numbered and showed us a symbol of Ponty. It was a nice plate and there was a little booklet in with information about Wilkinson's.

The cleanest feet in town

■ On Fridays we used to have to wash the floor in the starch room, by throwing buckets of hot water about. We then had to take our shoes off because our feet got wet through. We must have had the cleanest feet in town on Fridays.

I was always covered head to foot in starch and had to wash my hair every day. Sometimes we used to get round the back near the starch hole, where we couldn't be seen because of the pallettes, and have a cal and a bit of a lark about out of the forewoman's way.

■ Mr Harrison was the manager of Wilkinson's when I worked there. I have never seen anyone move around so quick as he did, every morning he would go all the way round the factory checking everything and everybody. He would run up the stairs from the spanish to the cream room, three steps at a time, and then to go back down he would slide down the bannister rail.

■ It was a long way from Wilkinson's to Knottingley crossroads but two old ladies used to walk to work every day. Maggie and Lizzie Kinsella worked in Wilkinson's factory. They were two sisters both well into their sixties and they used to pass by our house morning and evening.

Lizzie was slightly older and she would march smartly along; Maggie would try to keep up with her but it meant a little shuffly run every now and again. Lizzie never said much but Maggie always said, "Hello love" or, "Good morning."

They both must have worked well into their sixties but they never used the bus, they always walked.

■ Mrs Flynn's mum who would have been 104 now, worked for

67

The day Princess Margaret came to Wilkinson's

Addingley's, in Robinson's Yard near Walkergate in Pontefract. She bought a dinner service from Addingley's when their belongings were sold off after the family died. Mrs Flynn still has a plate from that dinner service.

■ From where I lived as a child you could smell Wilkinson's liquorice works if the wind was in the right direction. Sometimes there would be a lovely minty smell or a lovely creamy smell.

Walking along to school we could always check Wilkies clock to see if we were late or not. You could always guarantee their clock being right and, being high up, you could see the clock a long way off.

■ In the 1920s youngsters used to go to the factory doors at Dunhill's Tower Works, which is now the clothing factory in Southgate and Ewbank's, now the hospital work shop, and Addingley's which was situated at the back of Rington's Tea warehouse in Harrop Well Lane, to buy a 3d parcel of liquorice. You got about a pound - enough for the family.

■ Do you know how liquorice allsorts came to be called that? There was a bloke called Charlie Thompson who was a rep for Basset's in Sheffield before the first war. They reckon he'd had a good session on the beer one day and got all his samples mixed up. He couldn't get them sorted so the next place he visited he introduced his new line "liquorice allsorts." And that's true is that.

Adios amigos

ALL SORTS OF DIFFERENT TERMS

Feeding   Putting cream into the machine which made cream sheets

Stalking   Putting stalks into freshly made coconut mushrooms by hand

Stripping   Removing cakes, spanish sticks, spanish sheets etc, from boards after they had been in the stoves

Caking   Putting freshly made balls of liquorice onto a tray and stamping over each with a cake stamp

Jolloping   Brushing a form of sweet gum into sweets of cream and liquorice to make them stick together

Glazing   Dipping a hard juice into a brown liquid to give it a good shine

Cutter   A machinist who cuts up sheets of liquorice allsorts into cubes

Sweeper   A person who brushes sheets of cream, to remove the starch

Stacker   A person who stacks the trays of freshly made sweets

Nomping   Putting non-pareil balls onto freshly made jellies

'FEEDING' WOULD BE A BEGINNER'S FIRST JOB

THE NEW GIRL WHO THOUGHT THAT.....

STALKING MUSHROOMS MEANT A
DAY IN THE GARDENS!

WEIGHING 'BABIES' SOUNDED
A PLEASANT KIND OF JOB

'JOLLOPING' WAS A NEW SORT OF GAME

HAVING 'TO STRIP' IN THE STOVE
WAS GOING A LITTLE TOO FAR

MANUFACTURERS OF PONTEFRACT CAKE
AT THE TURN OF THE CENTURY

Taylor White	Friarwood
Ewbanks	Friarwood
Addingley	Harrop Well Lane
Dunhills	Broad Lane
Austerberry	Southgate
Horsfall	North Baileygate
Wheatley	North Baileygate
Hopkinson	Northgate
Sampson Gundhill	Finkle Street
Wilkinsons	Skinner Lane
Robinson and Wordsworth	Wordsworth Yard
Wheatley	Hardwick View
Hillabys	Back Street Tanshelf
Wilsons	Horsefair
Cowling	Nag's Head Yard

A FLAVOUR FOR DATES

1284   First written record of liquorice growing in England

1600   First reference to liquorice growing in Pontefract

1614   Evidence of the production of Pontefract Cakes for medicinal purposes, in the form of an apothecary's die-stamp

1648   Visual reference to Liquorice garths around Pontefract Castle

1701   Borough of Pontefract prohibited the sale of buds or sets outside the town to prevent a rival industry being set up in Knottingley

1760   George Dunhill first manufactured a sweetmeat by adding sugar to liquorice

1872   Dunhill die-stamp used to seal first secret ballot boxes in the by-election

1888   Mr Wilkinson opened up a factory - previously supplies came from the local inhabitants working in a cottage industry

1920   Pontefract was the last area in England to successfully grow liquorice commercially

1944   End of World War II saw a marked decline in the cultivation of liquorice

1966   Last commercial crop of liquorice was harvested by Wilkinson's

1990   Over 90% of the world crop is now used to flavour American tobacco. As the west becomes more affluent, it has turned to chocolate. Liquorice is still a popular sweet in developing countries

ART CIRCUS EDUCATION

Have you ever thought of being involved in producing a book like this one?

Art Circus Education offers courses for the first time writer as well as for people who want to learn how to use word processors and desk top publishing equipment.

The courses are free, practical and, what's more, you don't need any previous qualifications. What you do need is enthusiasm. If you want to learn to write, publish and sell your own books we have the course for you. And this isn't just training for the sake of it. The skills you learn are transferable, that means they might help you find a job or a place in further education.

If you have an interest in local stories, local history, writing, art and craft and want to take it step a further, give us a call at Yorkshire Art Circus - (0977) 550401 - and ask for Ian Clayton.

Courses planned for 1992/93 are in storytelling, word processing, spread sheets, data bases, desk top publishing, art and craft and business basics. Send for our brochure.